T/599.789
SUMMER 2011

PANDA RESCUE

PANDA RESCUE

Changing the Future for Endangered Wildlife

DAN BORTOLOTTI

FIREFLY BOOKS

A Firefly Book

Published by Firefly Books Ltd. 2003

First printing

PUBLISHER CATALOGING-IN-PUBLICATION DATA (U.S.)
(Library of Congress Standards)
Bortolotti, Dan.
Panda rescue : changing the future for endangered wildlife / Dan Bortolotti. —1st ed.
[64] p. : col. photos. ; cm.   (Firefly animal rescue)

Includes index and bibliographical references.
Summary: An exploration of pandas, their natural environment and in captivity, the threat of extinction,
and the conservationists who are working with them.
ISBN 1-55297-598-3
ISBN 1-55297-557-6 (pbk.)
1. Pandas—Juvenile literature. 2. Endangered species—Juvenile literature. I. Title. II. Series.
578.68 21 QL737.C214.B67 2003

NATIONAL LIBRARY OF CANADA CATALOGUING IN PUBLICATION DATA
Bortolotti, Dan
Panda rescue : changing the future for endangered wildlife / Dan Bortolotti.
(Firefly animal rescue)
Includes index.
ISBN 1-55297-598-3 (bound).—ISBN 1-55297-557-6 (pbk.)
1. Pandas—Juvenile literature. 2. Endangered species—Juvenile literature. I. Title. II. Series.
QL737.C214B67 2003   j599.789   c2003-902852-6

Published in the United States in 2003 by
Firefly Books (U.S.) Inc.
P.O. Box 1338, Ellicott Station
Buffalo, New York 14205

Published in Canada in 2003 by
Firefly Books Ltd.
3680 Victoria Park Avenue
Toronto, Ontario, M2H 3K1

Design: Ingrid Paulson
Maps: Roberta Cooke

Printed in Canada by Friesens, Altona, Manitoba

*The Publisher acknowledges the financial support of the Government of Canada through the
Book Publishing Industry Development Program for its publishing activities.*

TABLE OF CONTENTS

THE BEAUTY OF THE BEAST

No animal has made a more powerful impression on humanity in so little time.

In the West and even in its native China, the giant panda has been part of popular culture for less than a century. In North America, few had even seen a live panda before 1936, when one was exhibited at Chicago's Brookfield Zoo. But only a few decades later, the black-and-white bear had become the most beloved animal in the world, and an emblem of all endangered species.

According to George Schaller, the first Western scientist to study them, "There are two giant pandas: the one that exists in our mind and the one that lives in its wilderness home." It's true. Wild pandas are unimpressive in size and speed. They're unsociable and spend almost all their time eating, sleeping and defecating. Yet many people look into the panda's round face, with those expressive eyes, and declare it the most intriguing and lovable of creatures. The giant panda has charmed us with its simple, unique beauty.

In less than a century, the giant panda has become the world's most beloved animal.

But this beauty is fragile. Three million years ago, the panda's range extended throughout much of eastern China and into Myanmar (formerly Burma) and Vietnam. Today, with just over 1,000 remaining in the wild, the giant panda is one of the rarest of mammals, scratching out a living in a country of more than a billion people. If current trends continue—especially the destruction of its habitat—stuffed toys may be all that future generations will have left of these real-life teddy bears.

Fortunately, the Chinese—with the help of dedicated scientists and conservationists around the world—are beginning to reverse these trends.

< A giant panda bravely tests the strength of a thin branch in Wolong Nature Reserve. Pandas are among the world's rarest mammals, confined to just a handful of forests in three Chinese provinces.

WHERE DO PANDAS LIVE?

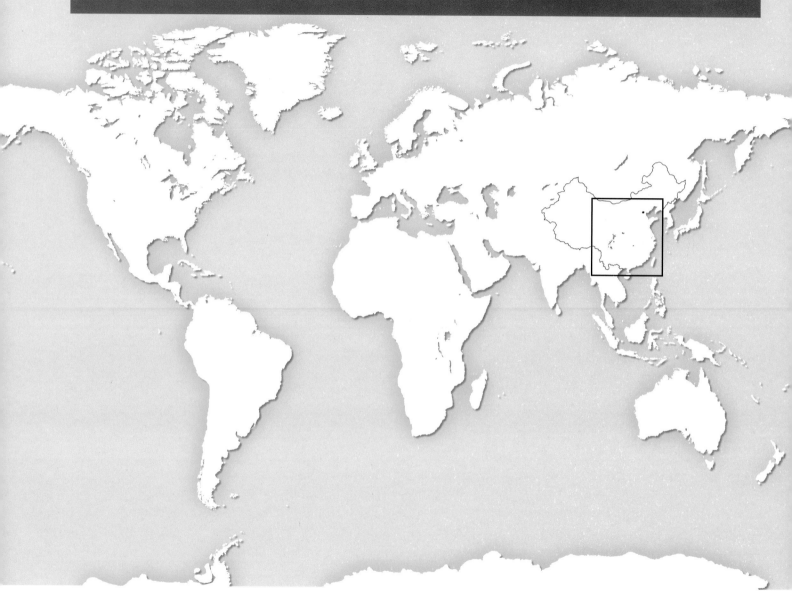

There at least 32 separate giant panda populations, covering six mountain ranges in three Chinese provinces: Sichuan, Gansu and Shaanxi. The biggest group, of perhaps 600 animals, lives in the Minshan Mountains in northern Sichuan. The Qinling Mountains to the northeast also host significant populations. Many other areas support only a handful of pandas.

THE STORY SO FAR

Before the mid–20th century, few people gave serious thought to protecting wild animals. By the 1960s, conservationists had begun to draw attention to the plight of endangered species, and almost immediately the giant panda moved to the top of that list.

China has since set up nature reserves to safeguard their land, though only about half of the wild population lives in these protected areas. Pandas are also protected by law from hunting, and poachers and smugglers can face life in prison.

∧ The research station in Wolong Nature Reserve.

1940s Chinese scientists begin observing the giant panda in the wild. Little is yet learned about its behavior.

1960s China creates the first four panda reserves. Hunting the animal is officially outlawed, as is exporting pelts.

1974 Scientists begin a two-year survey. When complete, it will estimate there are 2,500 pandas in the wild.

1975 The Wolong Nature Reserve is created in Sichuan. It is estimated to contain 145 pandas.

1979 World Wildlife Fund (WWF) and the Chinese government agree to the first international plan to save the giant panda.

1980 Eminent U.S. zoologist George Schaller joins Chinese scientists Hu Jinchu and Pan Wenshi to make a pioneering study of pandas in Wolong Nature Reserve.

1985 A new census begins. Three years later it suggests the number of pandas has shrunk to between 1,000 and 1,100.

1988 Authorities discover dozens of panda pelts for sale on the black market. Under pressure to get tough with poachers, China sentences 11 people to life in prison for the killing of two pandas.

1992 China adopts The National Conservation Programme for the Giant Panda and its Habitat, drawn up in 1989.

Shuan Shuan is one of several pandas born in Mexico City's Chapultepec Zoo, which runs a large breeding program. Most conservationists, however, believe that efforts should be focused on habitat protection.

1996   The Convention on International Trade in Endangered Species (CITES) speaks out against wild-caught animals being loaned to other countries, except when earnings can be channeled into conservation efforts.

1997   Conservationists meet at Wolong to discuss reintroducing captive pandas to the wild, concluding it is not yet possible. This same year, Chinese scientists begin experimenting with cloning.

1998   China bans commercial logging across most of the giant panda's habitat. The United States Fish and Wildlife Service adopts a policy governing panda loans to American zoos, ensuring the animals are not used solely for commercial gain.

2002   China creates five new giant-panda reserves in Shaanxi province, bringing the total number of reserves to 40.

LAND OF THE PANDA

The misty mountain forests of China are temperate, with lots of precipitation. Summers are mild and rainy, and fall brings beautiful colors. Light snow blankets the ground in winter before spring erupts with the blooms of more than 300 native species of rhododendron. These forests are also home to dozens of bamboo species that make up the panda's diet.

Pandas live at fairly high altitudes, moving from valley slopes as low as 5,000 feet (1,500 m) in winter to almost 12,000 feet (3,600 m) in summer. They share the landscape with many types of pheasant; primates, such as the golden monkey and Tibetan macaque; musk deer; spotted leopards; bamboo rats; and countless other animals.

While few of the panda's neighbors pose any serious danger, one species threatens its very existence: humans. Particularly in the last hundred years, people have pushed their way up the mountainsides, cutting timber and clearing land for crops. They've crowded pandas into smaller areas, cutting them off from other populations and sometimes leaving them with only one species of bamboo for food. With more than 85 million people living in Sichuan alone, it's a numbers game that the panda can't hope to win—unless humans are willing to level the playing field.

∧ The Minshan Mountains in Sichuan are home to China's largest panda population.

< The black-and-white fur of a panda stands out prominently against the earthy colors of the Wolong forest. Despite their distinctive markings, though, pandas are notoriously hard to spot in the wild.

IF A TREE FALLS IN THE FOREST...

Like so many other animals, the giant panda is endangered mainly because farming and logging have destroyed and fragmented much of its habitat.

China is the world's most populous country, with more than a billion people living there—a million humans for every panda. That's a lot of people who need land for growing food, and timber for building homes and for fuel. If these activities are properly managed—that is, if they involve limited cutting followed by replanting of trees—the situation will not necessarily spell doom. But many forests have been clear-cut: every single tree has been chopped down to make room for farming and grazing.

In 1998, the Chinese government banned commercial logging throughout the panda's range. But smaller-scale cutting continues, and even protected areas are not immune. People living near panda reserves sometimes enter them illegally to collect wood or graze their livestock.

In China, many forests have been clear-cut: every single tree has been chopped down.

In the Wolong Nature Reserve in Sichuan, home to one of the largest panda populations, more than 4,000 people actually live inside the protected area. Almost 250 acres (100 ha) of forest are cut down every year —more than four times the rate of destruction before Wolong was protected in 1975. In fact, between 1974 and 1989, the amount of suitable land for giant pandas in Sichuan was reduced by half as a growing number of farmers moved farther and farther up the mountains.

Illegal logging in Wolong Nature Reserve.

Why does this continue? Wildlife conservation is often at odds with economic development. People who have long made their living by farming and harvesting forest products tend to resist laws made without their involvement. And while the Chinese government now spends billions of dollars on wildlife conservation each year, in the past it was sometimes slow to make new policies and support them with funding. Finally, even where there are effective laws in place, they're not always enforced, since many of the staff who patrol the reserves are poorly trained and poorly paid, and can suffer from low morale. They may also be in the difficult position of enforcing laws that will harm people from their own villages.

S ometimes laws passed for one purpose have secondary benefits as well. That's the case with the 1998 law that halted logging throughout the giant panda's range. While the ban has certainly been good news for pandas and other wildlife, that wasn't its primary goal. Rather, it was to respond to massive floods in Sichuan.

Karen Baragona, manager of the giant panda conservation program for WWF, points out also that the prohibition is only supposed to last until 2010. "Long-term bans may not be feasible," she says, "so there needs to be a realistic plan to ensure the cutting that does go on in the future is sustainable."

Conservation organizations recognize that the most important player in this game is the Chinese government. It makes the laws, and it employs the rangers, scientists and staff who work in the reserves.

∧ Efforts to protect wildlife must also consider local people who share the land—and the bamboo—with pandas.

China has come up with an ambitious plan to convert some agricultural land back to grassland or forest. "Like the logging ban, it has far-reaching implications for giant panda conservation," Baragona explains. "It offers an unprecedented opportunity to restore habitat. WWF is working with the Chinese government to ensure that pandas come out ahead."

Finding enough money and competent, motivated staff is a continuing struggle. "Poor equipment and facilities are a major constraint," says Yu Changqing, who leads panda conservation programs for WWF China. To help out, WWF has trained hundreds of reserve staff and provided vehicles, funding and other support to the Chinese efforts.

< Every year, floods in China cause landslides that can kill hundreds of people. Cutting down forests in mountainous areas can create unstable slopes, which make landslides more likely.

AT WORK | COLBY LOUCKS

When Colby Loucks goes to work each day, he's a long way from the panda habitat he's working to protect. But the distance doesn't bother him. After all, he's got a good map.

Loucks is a senior conservation specialist with World Wildlife Fund in Washington, D.C. He has degrees in biology and environmental management, plus a more specialized skill: he's trained in geographic information systems (GIS), a technology that uses computers to combine maps and other information to create a detailed picture of a region.

In 1997, WWF China was looking for someone to identify what was left of the shrinking panda habitat in Qinling, a mountain range in Shaanxi province. "That's exactly what I had been trained to do," Loucks says. "I was really eager to apply my knowledge of both GIS and landscape ecology to an environmental problem."

First, he combined topographic maps (which show changes in elevation, like hills and valleys) with satellite images showing forests and nearby towns and roads. Then he plugged in information about where bamboo was found. "We began to get a sense of where the remaining habitat was for these pandas, and to see where the threats were. We combined this information with what researchers in the region already knew about where pandas lived, and we were able to make good predictions about what needed to be done in this mountain chain."

Of course, computers and maps are just tools, and the real power is in the person using them — so that person needs firsthand knowledge of the region. "I don't think you can make decisions from an office without ever going into the field," Loucks says. "I've visited Qinling, and every time I go to China I learn so much just talking to people and seeing the habitat."

Armed with a camera and a tempting piece of bamboo, Colby Loucks pays a visit to a baby panda in Wolong Nature Reserve. Conservationists in the West are inspired by seeing these animals in their native land.

Like most people in his line of work, Loucks is cautiously optimistic about the panda's future. He's encouraged by the attitude of the Chinese government in recent years, and says that the logging ban may give the panda some breathing room. "It gives conservationists several years to think about what to do once the ban is over. If we can collect some hard data and give an informed opinion to the Chinese government before 2010, then we might be able to protect the most important panda habitat. And if we can protect a decent amount of what's left, then pandas stand a good chance of being around in a hundred years."

"If we can collect some hard data and give an informed opinion to the Chinese government, then we might be able to protect the most important panda habitat."

A STAR IN THE EAST

Though the panda has only recently become a true Chinese emblem, ancient Chinese texts suggest that people have known about the giant panda for more than 2,000 years.

The animal was important to the Western Han Dynasty, which ruled China from 206 B.C. until A.D. 24. An emperor of that period kept an exotic zoo with many rare species, including a prized giant panda; and a royal tomb from this dynasty was discovered with a panda skull inside. During the Tang Dynasty (A.D. 618 to 907), China presented its Japanese neighbors with two pandas. It was a diplomatic tradition the country would repeat several times in the 20th century.

Some people suggest the panda's distinctive markings were a reason it appealed to rulers and thinkers. The contrasting black and white may have symbolized the yin and yang, the balancing forces in Chinese philosophy. But although the panda was familiar to the ruling classes of China, it doesn't seem to have impressed many early artists and writers. The poet Bai Juyi, in the eighth and ninth centuries, did mention the giant panda, endowing it with the power to ward off disaster and evil spirits. However, the animal rarely appeared in artwork or written texts before the 1900s. Perhaps the animal was simply too rare to have grabbed the attention of people in such a large country.

Many early texts refer only to a "white bear," and a Tibetan myth handed down through time suggests the panda might not always have had its black markings. One day, as the story goes, a young shepherdess was killed trying to protect a friendly panda from an attacking leopard. In mourning for the brave girl, the other pandas fashioned black armbands. As they wept for the shepherdess, they wiped their eyes, pulled on their ears and embraced one another. The black ashes made a pattern on the fur that the animal wears to this day.

THE PANDA GOES WEST

"I have not seen this species, which is easily the prettiest kind of animal I know, in the museums of Europe. Is it possible that it is new to science?"
— *Père Armand David, in a letter to the Paris Museum of Natural History, 1869*

1869   The body of an unknown animal is brought to Père Armand David, a Jesuit missionary and naturalist in China. He calls the animal *Ursus melanoleucus*, which means "black-and-white bear." The following year, David's colleague in France, Alphonse Milne-Edwards, declares the animal's skeleton to be more like a raccoon's than a bear's, and renames it *Ailuropoda melanoleucus*.

1916   German zoologist Hugo Weigold becomes the first Westerner to observe a live giant panda, when he purchases a cub from local villagers. He is unable to raise the cub, however, and it dies shortly afterward.

1929   Theodore and Kermit Roosevelt, sons of the former U.S. president, lead an expedition to China, sponsored by the Field Museum of Natural History in Chicago. They shoot a panda and bring it back to be exhibited at the museum.

1936   Ruth Harkness, a fashion designer from New York, organizes an unlikely expedition to China after her husband dies trying to capture a live panda for the Bronx Zoo. After weeks in the forest, Harkness's team emerges with Su Lin, a 3-pound (1.5-kg) cub that is eventually seen by two million people during its first year at Chicago's Brookfield Zoo. Harkness brings another panda to Brookfield in 1938, and the zoo acquires a third in 1939.

1941   The wife of Chinese statesman Chiang Kai-shek donates a panda pair to the American people, in gratitude for financial aid. Pan Dee and Pan Dah live at the Bronx Zoo until their deaths in 1945 and 1951, respectively.

1961 Sir Peter Scott, director of the recently launched World Wildlife Fund (WWF), chooses the panda as the organization's emblem. At the time, the London Zoo's Chi Chi is the only giant panda in the Western world.

1972 The Chinese government presents U.S. president Richard Nixon with two pandas for his part in improving relations between the two nations. Ling Ling and Hsing Hsing enjoy long lives at the Smithsonian National Zoo in Washington, D.C., and are closely studied by zoologists. Ling Ling dies in 1992 at age 23, while Hsing Hsing lives to be 28, dying in 1999.

1980s Dozens of pandas are taken from the wild—partly in an overzealous attempt to "rescue" cubs thought to be in danger, and partly to feed the demand for zoo pandas.

1981 Tohui, a female cub, is born at the Chapultepec Zoo in Mexico City. It is the first time a giant panda born outside China survives for more than a few days.

1996 The Zoological Society of San Diego and the Chinese government agree to a 12-year deal: the Americans will contribute $1 million annually to protect panda habitat, in exchange for the right to exhibit two pandas, Bai Yun and Shi Shi.

1999 Bai Yun gives birth to Hua Mei at the San Diego Zoo. She is the first panda born in the West in almost a decade.

∧ Hua Mei celebrates her third birthday at the San Diego Zoo in August 2002, complete with a cake and bamboo candles. Pandas are among the most popular attractions at zoos, where loving fans can follow every milestone.

2000 Mei Xiang and Tian Tian, who were born in captivity in China, arrive at the Smithsonian National Zoo, as part of a 10-year research and breeding program.

2003 Gao Gao—a male rescued from the wild in 1993 after suffering dehydration and injury—is loaned to the San Diego Zoo.

< Ruth Harkness brought the first giant panda to North America in 1936. Earlier in the year, her husband had died in Shanghai attempting the same feat.

THE IRONIC THREAT

The panda's beauty is an important reason why efforts to save it have such a high profile. Children break open their piggy banks to donate to panda conservation. Chinese citizens respond in droves when the animals appear threatened by a bamboo die-off. It's difficult to imagine the same effort directed at conserving the warthog or the wildebeest. And yet our love of the giant panda may, ironically, pose a threat of its own.

Some people believe the human fascination with pandas has occasionally led us to make poor decisions. Efforts to save an endangered species should be concentrated in the wild—that is, protecting the animal and its habitat from harm so that it can thrive as nature intended. But these projects are not dramatic; protecting a few hundred acres of forest might be good for the species, but it doesn't get into the newspapers. A single panda born in captivity, on the other hand, makes international headlines.

Research and breeding of captive animals plays a role in wildlife conservation, and in some cases it has saved species that certainly would have become extinct. But critics argue that too many giant pandas have been taken into captivity.

< Many were angered when Yingying, a 17-year-old captive-born panda, performed at a festival in Beijing, China, in 2001. Conservationists oppose the exploitation of endangered species in the entertainment industry.

About 150 pandas currently live in zoos and breeding centers, where they die faster than they can reproduce. Why so many? One reason is that people driven to save this species can make hasty judgments when a crisis comes along.

George Schaller reports that, during his study, a relatively minor bamboo die-off resulted in many animals being taken into captivity from areas where they faced no food shortage. Sometimes this was because rewards were offered.

Similarly, dozens of panda cubs have been taken out of the wild because they were thought to have been abandoned. Scientists now know that mothers leave their cubs for up to 40 hours while they go out to find food, and today these unnecessary rescues are less common than they were during the 1980s.

In the 1980s, people regularly removed panda cubs from the wild in the mistaken belief that they had been abandoned by their mothers. >

PANDAS IN CAPTIVITY

Conservationists agree that protecting the panda's disappearing habitat is their top priority. Still, research on captive animals, both in China and in the West, can play an important role in the long-term survival of the species.

Exhibiting pandas outside China has always been controversial. No other animal attracts so many visitors and so much money, and many foreign zoos have clamored for pandas. Today, loans are strictly regulated to make sure the animals are not exploited for profit. Pandas can only be imported for long-term research, and money raised from exhibiting them is directed back to China to protect habitats. In the United States, each zoo exhibiting pandas contributes $1 million (U.S.) annually, usually for 10 years or more.

∧ A two-week-old panda whines inside an incubator at Chengdu Research Base, one of the largest breeding centers in China.

Pandas are notoriously difficult to study in the wild, so research on captive animals can help conservationists better understand panda behavior and apply that knowledge to their work in the field.

In the past, Western critics argued that researchers across the ocean were disorganized and uncooperative, but that's beginning to change. "The communication between China and the West is one of the most encouraging signs in panda conservation," says Rebecca Snyder, coordinator of giant panda research at Zoo Atlanta. She also points out that zoos in the U.S. must share their research, as part of their loan agreements.

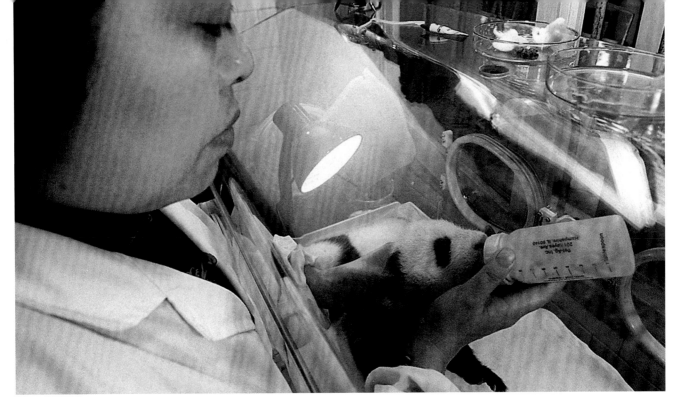

A veterinarian feeds a 40-day-old baby panda at Chengdu Research Base. Studying captive animals can help conservationists protect them in the wild, but breeding pandas has proven to be very difficult.

If the hurdles of breeding can be overcome, captive-born giant pandas may someday be reintroduced to the wild. Experts agree, though, that this is a long way from becoming reality.

> "In a lot of ways, pandas are good candidates," Rebecca Snyder explains. "They don't have to learn to hunt, the adults have no predators and their food is abundant in good habitat." But, she continues, scientists first need to know if the shrinking forests in China could sustain more animals without causing competition. She also points out that pandas being prepped for release in the wild would need to be raised very differently from the way they are now. They would have to learn to find food on their own, and cubs would need to remain with their mothers for much longer.

As a young girl growing up in Iowa, Rebecca Snyder thought pandas were cute and charming, but she never dreamed about working with them. Even later, while studying psychology and animal behavior at the Georgia Institute of Technology in Atlanta, her earliest research was on tigers. Then, while pursuing her doctorate, Snyder got the opportunity to work at the second-largest panda breeding center in the world.

"I got excited about the thought of going to China," says Snyder. She worked on and off in Chengdu for two years, observing the center's population of about two dozen pandas. That's where she got hooked. "Once you spend any time around pandas, they're very magnetic. They really have this effect on you."

∧ In 1999, United Parcel Service delivered Lun Lun and Yang Yang to Zoo Atlanta by "Panda Express."

Snyder's research has focused on the panda's reproductive behavior and the relationship between mothers and cubs. Scientists doing this work have to be observant, meticulous and patient. While studying breeding habits, for example, Snyder sits outside the animals' enclosure with a pencil and a clipboard. Each time she observes a female panda displaying a behavior like scent marking, or a vocalization like bleating or chirping, she makes note of it. In order to get reliable data, Snyder and her colleagues often observe for eight hours a week, nine months a year, for several years. Eventually, the research is published and shared with other scientists and conservationists.

Rebecca Snyder observes captive pandas at both Zoo Atlanta and Chengdu. Cooperation between scientists in Asia and the West is an encouraging sign in panda conservation, she says.

Today, as curator of giant panda research and management at Zoo Atlanta, Snyder keeps a watchful eye over Lun Lun and Yang Yang, who are on loan from China. The zoo maintains close ties with the research center in Chengdu, sharing resources and expertise, and Snyder is impressed by China's growing interest in conservation.

"The people I work with in China truly care about the panda and its future," she says. "For many of them, seeing that the species is preserved has been a lifelong ambition. The panda has instilled a sense of international cooperation that I haven't seen with any other species. It's encouraging to see how such a quiet, unassuming animal can inspire all these people."

"Once you spend any time around pandas, they're very magnetic," says Rebecca Snyder. "They really have this effect on you."

PANDA PLAY

Few people can resist the sight of pandas at play. In captivity, panda cubs and their mothers may play for a couple of hours a day, in spurts of up to 20 minutes at a time. They enjoy rough-and-tumble activities—biting, play fighting, pawing and chasing one another.

Scientists aren't sure why captive pandas play and they don't know how widespread this behavior is in the wild, where mothers are usually busy foraging. Other than the occasional climbing and tumbling of infants, there isn't much evidence of playful behavior outside captivity. During his lengthy study in Wolong, George Schaller reports, "We had no opportunity to observe play in the wild," although he watched a panda slide down a snowy hill—something that grizzly bears also do—when it likely could have walked more easily. Chinese researchers have observed play between mothers and cubs, too, but at a much lower level than in captivity.

Like so much about the giant panda, its playful behavior is often misunderstood. As Schaller writes, "Pandas project such charm and vulnerability that people tend to see only the image, not the animal — a panda is powerful, potentially dangerous, and its moods are understated." In fact, Schaller says, in proportion to the number of captive animals, only elephants cause more serious injuries.

∧ Hua Mei frolics in artificial snow at the San Diego Zoo. Captive pandas have more opportunity to play than their wild counterparts.

While few people have observed pandas playing in the wild—they're usually too busy feeding—they have been known to have a little fun. This panda was caught sliding down a snowy slope in Wolong.   >

ITS OWN WORST ENEMY?

Another misguided notion about the panda paints it as a bumbling, clownish creature that just isn't up to the task of surviving in the wilderness. This idea may come from watching panda cubs—either in zoos or on film—struggling to climb a tree, or lolling about like playful house pets that wouldn't last in the harsh forest.

Some people feel the panda might be doomed by nature.

In addition, many have argued that the species is heading toward an evolutionary dead end. Some feel that the panda's overspecialized diet of bamboo will eventually lead to its natural extinction. Others mistakenly believe that the animal is unable to properly look after its young.

The Times of London has reported that the panda is "one of a group of survivors of the last ice age that has been slowly dying off as their habitats contract naturally." And the former editor of China's *Great Nature* magazine has written, "Just as all living creatures go through three different phases— birth, development and decline—so has the panda species. The giant panda has entered its decline." Even if we were to protect pandas and their habitat, the thinking goes, it wouldn't make a difference in the long run.

These arguments frustrate conservationists, who believe we must accept that the panda's main threats are saws and snares, not the animal's own nature. Only then will humans be able to come up with a realistic plan to save the species.

Suggesting pandas are doomed by nature also makes captive breeding seem more attractive, despite its limited success. As a result, breeding programs may receive money and resources that might otherwise go to protecting pandas in the wild.

< The panda's bumbling appearance has led to the mistaken belief that it's ill-equipped to survive in the wilderness. But conservationists know that its greatest enemy is not nature, but human activity.

PANDAS INSIDE OUT

The giant panda spends almost all its waking hours feeding. To understand why, it helps to know a little about how the body turns food into energy. Meat is rich in protein and other nutrients that are easily absorbed, so carnivores usually have a simple digestive system— a basic stomach, followed by relatively short intestines. Plants are much harder to digest, so animals who eat them rely on a few tricks. Some, like horses and elephants, have a large sac near the end of their digestive tracts where plant food is stored while microbes break it down. Others, like cattle, can partially digest food before regurgitating it and chewing it again. In general, plant-eating animals have much longer intestines, too, so the food passes through the body more slowly.

Pandas have a vegetarian diet and a meat eater's body.

Giant pandas, however, have a vegetarian's diet and a meat eater's body. Like bears, they have a short, uncomplicated digestive tract with few microbes to break down tough plant material. And yet their diet consists almost entirely of bamboo, a woody grass that is very low in nutrients and is about as easy to digest as a handful of chopsticks.

How does the panda deal with a food that would tear our bellies to shreds? For starters, its stomach and intestines are lined with thick walls of mucus that protect it from the shards of bamboo passing through its system. And they pass through quickly: from the time a panda swallows a meal, it's only about eight hours before it exits at the other end. When a panda eats, it uses its back teeth to break bamboo into pieces about an inch or two (2 to 5 cm) long. It chews each stem only five to nine times, which is very little considering how tough bamboo can be. But this is typical behavior: a panda won't waste effort on unnecessary chewing.

Pandas have evolved a unique bit of anatomy to help them process all that bamboo. Scientists call it an elongated radial sesamoid. Everyone else calls it a thumb.

The giant panda's forepaws have five digits (or fingers), but unlike in humans, these are lined up in a row. Using an extra-large wrist bone like a thumb, the panda can clutch items as small as a drinking straw. The added dexterity means the animal can eat bamboo more quickly, all the while using less of its precious energy.

THE PICKIEST EATER

Giant pandas in the wild don't eat just bamboo. They have been observed feeding on more than 20 kinds of plants, and they may even scavenge the kills of carnivores. However, all these other types of food make up only 1 percent of the panda's diet. The other 99 percent is bamboo, bamboo, bamboo.

99% of a panda's diet is bamboo, bamboo, bamboo.

Given the rich variety of plant life in their habitat, most of which is far more nutritious than this woody grass, why is the panda such a fussy eater? There are several reasons, the most important of which is availability. Where pandas live, bamboo is one of the most common plants. It's also evergreen, making it easy to find, even in light snow. And few other animals bother with it, the notable exceptions being the red panda— a raccoonlike relative of the giant panda—and the bamboo rat. All of this adds up to its being a plentiful food source that's available year-round.

Although the foliage is the most nutritious part of the bamboo plant, pandas don't just collect and eat leaves. They eat the shoots and stems as well, although the amount of each changes according to the season. From April to June, pandas feed mainly on the new shoots that are just emerging from the ground. From July to October, they eat almost exclusively leaves, and from November until spring they eat primarily the stems.

Pandas do not drink often, particularly when their diet is rich in shoots, since these supply them with more water than they need. At other times, they may visit a stream or pond up to four times a day.

To free up both its forepaws for holding and breaking bamboo, the panda usually sits down while eating, another of its endearing habits. Once it's finished, though, it's back to work. Just to get enough calories to survive, the giant panda must eat 22 to 40 pounds (10 to 18 kg) of bamboo every day.

∧ The red panda is the giant panda's closest relative and one of its few competitors for bamboo.

< Pandas often sit while eating in order to conserve energy and free up its forepaws. Bamboo is so poor in nutrients that the animal must eat up to 40 pounds (18 kg) each day to get enough calories.

BAMBOOZLED

Bamboo has a bizarre characteristic that poses a serious threat to the animals relying on it for food. Like many other plants, bamboo spreads itself by sending roots underground, emerging elsewhere as new shoots. And like all grasses, it also reproduces by flowering and generating new seeds. However, instead of doing this every year, most species of bamboo have extremely long and unpredictable flowering cycles, lasting from 30 to 120 years. When their time comes, all the plants of a given species flower simultaneously, and then die. It takes years for the new seedlings to mature and again become a viable food source for pandas.

In a vast forest uninhabited by humans, this would not necessarily be a problem. When one species of bamboo dies back, pandas could simply switch their diets to a different species, or move to a different area. This would even benefit them, since it would force populations to mingle. However, many panda populations are now surrounded by open farmland that pandas cannot cross, and some of these islands of forest contain just one type of bamboo. If this dies, pandas in these regions may starve.

If all the bamboo in a region dies back, pandas may starve.

One of the most dramatic bamboo die-offs occurred in the mid-1970s, when at least three bamboo species in northern Sichuan flowered and went to seed around the same time. About 150 pandas in the area starved to death. The tragedy was a wake-up call for the Chinese, and they responded in 1975 by creating the Wolong Nature Reserve, followed by several other protected areas and research projects.

Without the freedom to roam the forests and change food sources, however, pandas remain vulnerable to the quirky reproductive habits of bamboo.

Arrow bamboo is one of the species preferred by pandas in Wolong. Occasionally, > all of its plants flower, produce seeds and die back. The last time this happened, in 1983, dozens of pandas starved.

As they hone their long-term conservation plans, scientists need up-to-date information about where panda populations live and how many individuals there are.

In 1998, WWF researchers began a three-year survey to get the clearest picture they could. Colby Loucks explains how they do it: "Survey teams are made up of about 40 people, and they partition an area into two-square-kilometer blocks. Then they move through it looking for signs of pandas: droppings, feeding or den sites, scratchings and, very rarely, visual contact." Very rarely, indeed. "In three thousand man-days of field work, only two pandas were actually seen," he says. "That means the average person could spend four years in the field looking for pandas and only see one."

The most prevalent sign is panda droppings, Loucks says. "Pandas digest very little of what they eat, so the droppings contain large pieces of undigested bamboo. The teams pick these pieces from the droppings and measure them. The average bite size of the bamboo pieces is determined, and can then be compared with other droppings. If they're different bite sizes, then they're from different pandas. This gives us the best estimate of the minimum number of pandas left in the wild."

Matt Durnin, a panda researcher with the University of California, Berkeley, also examines bite lengths in his census work, but he's experimenting with a new method: DNA analysis. In addition to droppings, he collects hair samples by setting up barbed-wire snares that harmlessly snag fur from passing pandas. He then examines these samples to determine their unique genetic fingerprint, something that promises to be more accurate than bite-mark analysis.

∧ Droppings contain undigested bits of bamboo that may be used to identify and count pandas.

< Researchers in Wanglang Nature Reserve examine signs of panda presence. Since the animals are so elusive, scientists have developed methods of counting giant pandas without ever seeing them.

NUMBERS GAME

Since the groundbreaking studies in Wolong in the 1980s, virtually every book and article about pandas has set the wild population at about a 1,000 animals. The truth is that no one really knows how accurate that number is. Counting wild animals is difficult in the best of conditions, but it's especially challenging when dealing with solitary animals in remote, mountainous forests.

WWF completed the fieldwork for its panda census in November 2001 and found that the population had not declined below 1,000 animals.

Karen Baragona of WWF cautions against getting hung up on these numbers. "The purpose isn't just to count heads," she explains. "It's to get the clearest possible snapshot of where we are now—the size and distribution of the population and the extent of available or potential habitat—so we can monitor, and respond to, trends in the future. The survey will also show where important panda habitat is still unprotected, where new reserves should be established, and which areas should be priorities for forest restoration."

Matt Durnin agrees that the exact figure is not important. "Whether there's eight hundred pandas or two thousand—on a national scale, that's still small. What's important is that we monitor trends. There are certainly some populations that are remaining stable, and the smaller ones are declining."

George Schaller attaches a radio collar to a panda in Wolong Nature Reserve in >
the 1980s. Radio telemetry — that is, fitting wild animals with collars that can be tracked by researchers — has not been used to study pandas since 1995.

Matt Durnin has spent years studying pandas in Wolong Nature Reserve, living for months at a time in thin-walled wooden shacks without electricity or running water. But he recalls one night when returning to camp felt like checking into a luxury hotel.

Durnin and his research partner had set out to visit their camera traps on a cold, damp March day in 1999. When they realized it would be dark in an hour, they were still 3 miles (5 km) from camp. "The terrain is so difficult," Durnin says of Wolong. "It can take hours to get through just a couple of kilometers. I can't tell you how many times I wished I had a hang glider."

The two men were on a ridge several hundred yards from camp when the forest grew so dark they had to feel for the trail with their hands. "If I made one wrong move I would fall 15 or 20 feet to the rocks below," Durnin says. "At this point I knew we were in a precarious situation." No sooner had the thought crossed his mind than he slipped, but he fell only a few feet without injury. After that, they were reduced to shuffling along on their behinds until they were only about 50 yards (45 m) from home. "Here the trail was covered with rocks and boulders and was nearly vertical." There was no way to do it without a light, so they shouted down to the camp. "After about 20 minutes, our cook heard our cries and was off to rescue us."

< In three years in the field, Matt Durnin spotted just one wild panda. Here he takes a break with an eight-month-old at the research station in Wolong Nature Reserve.

> The terrain is so difficult in Wolong. "I can't tell you how many times I wished I had a hang glider."

Though not usually quite so harrowing, the life of a panda researcher in Wolong means long stretches in the remote wilderness. Each year from 1998 to 2001, Durnin spent six to eight months there, setting off each day with his Chinese colleagues to look for panda feces, hair and den sites. These are tough to find, he says, but with experience it becomes easier to notice even subtle signs of panda presence, such as flattened patches of bamboo. After many months of identifying individual pandas by what they leave behind, he can estimate the number of animals in a given area, where they've traveled, and how much they've mingled. "I can start to *see* populations."

For six years, Durnin and his wife Stephanie lived in China, where he learned to speak Mandarin, though "just enough to get me into trouble." He has concentrated on pandas since 1994, when he met Pan Wenshi and Hu Jinchu, two of China's most respected panda researchers. "To meet two scientists so dedicated to protecting and understanding giant pandas was really an honor and an inspiration. I still keep in touch with both of them and share my findings whenever I can."

Durnin recently earned his doctorate in wildlife ecology from the University of California, Berkeley, though he still travels to China to conduct fieldwork. And now he remembers to pack a flashlight.

∧ At Durnin's field site, he checks his camera trap (*top*), which photographs passing pandas; and a barbed-wire snare (*bottom*), which captures fur samples for genetic analysis.

THE SKIN TRADE

Panda pelts were given as royal gifts in ancient times, and killing the animal for its unique fur has a long history. In the early 1900s, panda pelts appeared on European floors as expensive rugs. Around the same time, Western writers in China reported that trapping pandas for their skins was widespread. As far back as 1946, a Hong Kong newspaper declared they might soon be hunted to extinction.

It's difficult to know how much of a market there is for panda skins today, but some of the evidence is alarming. In one 1988 crackdown, Chinese authorities seized 146 pelts in Sichuan. Other investigations have turned up much smaller numbers, but the skin trade appears to be continuing. Some reports claim that in Japan, Taiwan and other Asian countries, a single pelt can sell for $10,000 to $40,000 (U.S.) — perhaps much more.

The panda is given the highest level of protection under the law.

When the first studies began in Wolong, no one really knew how much poaching was still going on. Hunting for any reason is illegal in wildlife reserves, of course, but the promise of big money means that people are willing to take risks. So much so that a zoologist who worked in China in the late 1980s reports that "at the time, poaching was considered the single biggest threat to pandas."

Today, even if anti-poaching patrols are not as effective as they could be, the Chinese government takes trapping seriously. The panda is given the highest level of protection under the law, and the penalties for killing or trying to sell one is a lengthy prison term—some poachers have even been executed. This is enough to scare off many would-be panda smugglers.

∧ Pandas are sometimes killed in traps set for other animals, particularly musk deer like this one, who are valued for their scent glands. Poachers fit saplings with wire snares that strangle the unsuspecting animals, causing a slow and painful death.

Like so many other endangered species, giant pandas share their habitat with growing human populations, and both may compete for the same resources. Recently, China has made progress in tilting the balance in favor of pandas. There are now 40 reserves in the network —more than double what there were in the early 1990s—and there are plans to protect even more land. Perhaps more important is the 1998 temporary ban on logging in virtually all areas where pandas live.

But there are still problems. When a reserve is set up, farmers and villagers nearby are often prevented from using land they once relied on for food and timber. "The farmers are very cooperative, though they sometimes resent the limits placed on their activities," explains Yu Changqing of WWF China. "Sometimes, there are misunderstandings between conservationists and the farmers."

Even within nature reserves, where hunting, cutting and gathering are all prohibited, habitat may still be vulnerable, since people enter the reserves unlawfully. "Certainly there is some conflict between patrols and people who conduct illegal activities, such as poaching and bamboo-shoot collecting," says Yu.

Things are even more difficult when panda habitat lies outside the reserves. Conservationists are quick to point out that most farmers are not opposed to protecting wildlife. They're simply trying to earn a living and feed their families, who may have lived on this land as long as the pandas have. But in order to protect endangered animals, farming and other human activity must be limited —even outside of the nature reserves.

A smuggler's vehicle is captured in Wolong Nature Reserve with a load of illegal timber.

With this in mind, WWF is leading a program in Pingwu, a county in Sichuan. Among its 180,000 people live at least two hundred pandas, more than in any other county. But most of their habitat is not protected, and timber sales were once the main source of revenue in the region. "We're looking at helping the people in Pingwu develop other sources of income," says Karen Baragona of WWF. Together with the government and community leaders, WWF is promoting alternatives to logging, including ecotourism and the collection of forest products such as mushrooms and honey.

SPLENDOR IN THE BAMBOO

One of the greatest myths about pandas is that they have difficulty reproducing in the wild, and that this trait threatens their numbers. In truth, it's only in captivity that they reproduce reluctantly.

∧ A few days before giving birth, an expectant panda will find a suitable den and line it with leaves and branches.

All adult wild pandas appear to be active breeders — in comparison, just over a quarter of captive animals will breed. Research on wild populations has found that panda females give birth to an average of three cubs every two years. That doesn't sound like many, but it's enough to sustain the panda's numbers. After all, it has been doing just that for three million years.

Pandas are choosy about their mates — they must first determine whether there is any chemistry between them. If a female decides to reject a suitor, she will flee, even climbing a tree to escape. It's common for more than one male to approach a female, but in the end the highest-ranking male — that is, the largest or strongest — usually gets the female.

Baby pandas are born in late August or early September, and the litter is most often just a single cub. When twins are born, the weaker one dies soon after, since the mother simply does not have the resources to rear two at the same time.

Although pandas generally breed well in the wild, they do face potential problems because of their small, isolated populations. All mammals need genetic diversity to remain strong. As habitats become cut off from one another, animals may be forced to mate with close relatives. Inbreeding tends to make animals less fertile and more vulnerable to disease and defects. The good news: recent studies show that this is not yet a major problem for pandas.

A BREED APART

While Chinese scientists and conservationists are working hard to protect panda habitat, they also devote a great deal of time and money to breeding pandas in captivity. These attempts have had limited success.

∧ A veterinarian tends to a newborn panda cub. Captive-born pandas are highly vulnerable to infection and many survive for only a few months.

Giant pandas don't seem to like an audience when they mate. They're also selective: you can't put just any male and female together and expect them to produce a family. Mating behaviors appear to be learned in the wild, and captive pandas — particularly males — seem less than fluent in the language of love. Females only go into heat once a year, and cubs are so tiny and fragile that they often die of infections.

All of this helps to explain why, between 1936 and 1999, only about a hundred captive-born pandas have lived for more than a year. In 2002, only about a dozen were born in Chinese breeding centers.

At the Chengdu Research Base of Giant Panda Breeding, researchers are experimenting with ways of helping the process along. When females go into heat, scientists collect sperm from males and use it for artificial insemination — in other words, the sperm is deposited into the uterus of the female in an effort to make her pregnant. Almost all captive-born pandas are conceived this way.

A lab assistant at the Chengdu Research Base analyzes a sample of panda sperm. Captive pandas are notoriously reluctant to breed naturally, so almost all are born through artificial insemination.

Some scientists in China are also experimenting with cloning, a highly controversial technique. Even if cloning pandas were possible—and so far, it isn't—most experts argue strongly that it would do nothing to protect the species. Pandas may already be threatened by a lack of genetic diversity, a problem cloning would make worse. And with no evidence that it's possible to release captive-born animals into the wild, conservationists insist that money spent on questionable schemes like cloning would be better spent protecting habitat.

Even if cloning pandas were possible, most experts believe it would do nothing to protect the species.

AT WORK | LUO LAN

The city of Chengdu teems with over 10 million people—more than live in Los Angeles or New York. But if you drive just 6 miles (10 km) from this metropolis, heading north along Panda Road, you'll find hundreds of acres of bamboo, trees, flowers—and one of the most important centers in China for studying giant pandas.

∧ Luo Lan teaches Chinese children how to help protect pandas.

You'll also find Luo Lan, who works as a conservation educator at the Chengdu Research Base of Giant Panda Breeding.

Luo Lan studied mechanical technology in university, and until 1994 she worked as a technician in a factory. Then at age 26 she was offered a job at the Chengdu research center. "I hesitated to quit my job in a chemical plant, but the dream of working in a park was so strong and tempting. I decided to take it at last."

After three years as a guide, she spent three more as a research coordinator, observing panda behavior and helping scientists summarize the results. Today she travels to schools to spread her message to teachers and students of all ages, answering their questions about animals and how to protect them. "Conservation education is a bridge between people and pandas. I worry when people misunderstand the giant panda—a lot of people still think they are lazy or not smart. As a matter of fact, pandas are very smart. They just live a different lifestyle and schedule than we do."

Luo Lan is also helping to survey the people of Sichuan to hear their attitudes about conservation. "We need to understand how people feel about wildlife so we can provide relevant education."

What keeps her motivated? "I feel I must help giant pandas, not just because they live only in China, but also because whenever they look at me, the innocence and peace in their eyes always touch my heart."

55

WHAT IS THE PANDA'S FUTURE?

The panda's situation is still critical. But it's far from hopeless. In fact, progress in recent years has made many conservationists optimistic.

They point to several advances made since the late 1990s. First, the newly completed census will help scientists and governments identify problems and measure any improvement. A growing concern for environmental issues in China has led to better law enforcement and more emphasis on protecting and restoring forests. There's now more cooperation between Chinese and Western scientists than ever before. And stricter conditions on panda loans to overseas zoos mean the big money they attract will be used to protect them in the wild.

Scientists working with pandas both wild and captive have tried hard to dispel the myths about what threatens them. Their efforts should lead to money and resources flowing in the right directions.

The animal also has an ace in the hole: its status as one of the world's most beloved creatures. If any animal has the charisma to win over the world, it's the giant panda.

FAST FACTS

Scientific name	• *Ailuropoda melanoleuca*
Size	• length up to 6 feet (180 cm), height up to 3 feet (90 cm)
	• weight ranges from 185 to 275 pounds (85 to 125 kg)
	• males weigh 10 to 20 percent more than females
Life span	• 18 to 20 years in the wild
	• 30 or more in captivity
Locomotion	• walks on all fours in plantigrade fashion, meaning the entire sole of the foot touches the ground
	• gait appears clumsy, but moves easily through dense vegetation and steep slopes
	• an excellent tree climber
Social life	• solitary
	• avoids other pandas except when ready to mate or when mothers are tending their cubs
	• confined to home ranges of about 2 to 4 square miles (4 to 6 km²), depending on availability of bamboo
	• not territorial

Senses and Communication

- scent is most important method of communication; rubs trees with its scent glands (located between the anus and the genitals) to convey its age and sex, where it has been, how long ago it left and, in the case of females, its willingness to mate

- visual cues rare, since contact with other pandas is unusual and eyesight not acute

- relies on posture when necessary, lowering its head to look threatening

- limited vocabulary—snorting, growling, bleating, chirping and other sounds—used when courting a mate, or for communication at close range

Paws

- forepaws have five digits and a thumblike wrist bone adapted for eating bamboo

- digits on both front and back paws point inward when walking

Teeth

- 42 teeth, following the basic dental pattern of carnivores but with flat, wide molars and premolars adapted for grinding bamboo

- teeth set in a massive, muscular jaw so strong it can chew through metal

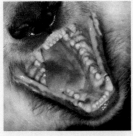

Reproduction

- reaches sexual maturity during sixth or seventh spring

- usually mates between March and May

- female in heat for 12 to 25 days a year

- gestation varies widely, from three to five months

- litter usually a single cub, averaging just 4 ounces (115 g)

HOW YOU CAN HELP

If you would like to learn more about giant pandas or the projects designed
to protect them, contact one the following organizations:

World Wildlife Fund U.S.
www.worldwildlife.org

1250 Twenty-Fourth Street N.W., P.O. Box 97180
Washington, D.C. U.S.A. 20090-7180
Phone (800) CALL-WWF

Features online fact sheets about pandas and other endangered species,
electronic postcards, and a free Action Kit offer (U.S. only).

World Wildlife Fund Canada
www.wwfcanada.org

245 Eglinton Avenue East, Suite 410, Toronto, ON, Canada M4P 3J1
Phone (800) 26-PANDA or (416) 489-8800

Offers online tips on getting involved in conservation efforts,
as well as classroom activities.

For more information about pandas, visit these Web sites:

Everything You Need to Know About the Giant Panda   *www.giantpandabear.com*

Zoo Atlanta   *www.zooatlanta.org*

Smithsonian National Zoo   *www.nationalzoo.si.edu*

San Diego Zoo   *www.sandiegozoo.org*

Chengdu Research Base of Giant Panda Breeding   *www.panda.org.cn*

INDEX

PHOTO CREDITS

AUTHOR'S NOTE

This book is dedicated with love to my daughter Jaimie.

The scientists and conservationists I interviewed for this book were extraordinarily generous. I am particularly indebted to Rebecca Snyder and Don Reid, who reviewed the manuscript and made many helpful suggestions.

Thanks also to Karen Baragona, Sarah Bexell, Matt Durnin, Colby Loucks, Luo Lan, Charles Rowland, Yu Changqing and Kerry Zobor.